GOD'S DAD JOKES COLORING BOOK

A COLORFUL WAY TO LEARN SCRIPTURE

RECORDED BY S.S. COULTER
ILLUSTRATED BY FERNANDO MEDINA

ISBN: 978-1-959568-15-5
SSCoulter.com

In January 2025, I was in prayer when I felt God move me to write a joke book. A joke book? I had seen many Dad Joke Books for sale, and I guess it was time for the Heavenly Father to join in on the fun! From that moment, I was inundated with God's Dad Jokes. I would be in my prayer closet laughing as more and more jokes came. I'd watch TV and have to write them down. I'd be reading my Bible … the jokes were everywhere! In just two short, joy-filled weeks, I had written down over 100 jokes!

I still have my childhood Bible. It has a picture of Jesus smiling on it; a picture that captured my heart when I was a little girl. Although the Jesus I would see at church services was usually somber and serious, the Jesus I had in my heart was happy and, yes, even FUNNY! God is infinite, and He made each of us in His image, uniquely created to reveal different parts of His Character to one another. I hope this book gives you a little glimpse into the part of Jesus who smiles, laughs, and loves to tell a good "bad dad" joke.

May God shine His smiling face upon your laughter.

S. S. Coulter

HELLO, FRIENDS!

Throughout this coloring book, you'll find some fun activities you can do. For more activities like these, please visit The Planet Fassa by scanning the QR code with your smart device.

Planet Fassa

SCAN ME!

When you enter The Planet Fassa, you enter a world of:

Fun   Activities   Stories   Service   Awards

We hope to see you there! Planet Fassa's Vision: **Together, nurturing hearts, strengthening minds, and moving bodies to change the world.**

Want more of God's Dad Jokes? Our original joke book contains the jokes in this coloring book, plus dozens more!

God's Dad Joke Book

SCAN ME!

This book belongs to:

_____

_____

Re-Name that ANIMAL

In Genesis, God asked Adam to name all the animals. In our joke on page 23, we pretended that Adam picked a human name like "Bob," but really, Adam picked the names for the *kinds* of animals like giraffe, dog, cat, and all the other ones. How cool! Now it's time to use your imagination to choose your own names for different kinds of animals!

WHAT YOU NEED
1. Paper
2. Coloring utensils
3. Writing utensil

DIRECTIONS

1. Think of your favorite animals. Do you like elephants, squirrels, or monkeys? Whatever you choose, write down five.

2. Now it's time for you to rename those animals.

3. Think about each animal:

   - What does it look like?
   - What sounds does it make?
   - What color is it?
   - Does it have big or small ears?
   - Does it have a short or long tail?
   - Does it have a big or small nose?
   - Does it have whiskers?
   - Is it soft or furry or slimy?

4. You can write down your answers to the questions or draw a picture of each animal – whatever you'd like to do!

5. Now look at your answers or drawings and think of ways to give each animal a *new* name. You are going to *re*-name them! There are many ways you can do this. Here are some ideas:

   - Look at your answers or drawings, pick something that really stands out to you, and make that the new name. For instance, since cats purr, you can rename them "Purrs." Or you can pick two things that stand out about them and call them "Fur Purrs"!

   - Another way to rename your animals is to take two or three of your answers (or three things you drew), write them down, and combine a few letters of each to come up with a name.

     Here are two examples:

     – **Cats**. Cats have fur, they purr, and they have whiskers. We can take the first few letters of each of those words (**fu**r, **pu**rr, **whi**skers), and call them Fupuwhi!

Planet Fassa

For more activities like this, please **SCAN ME!**

   – **Elephants**. They are **gra**y, have **tru**nks, and are **bi**g. We can call them Gratrubi!

   - A third thing you can do is just come up *with any new name YOU like!* Have you always wanted to call moneys, "Daydos"? Well then name them Daydos! It's up to you!

6. Write down all the new names you imagine! If you drew your animals, put their new names on the drawings, and hang them up for all to enjoy!

EXTRA CHALLENGES

1. Make it a game! Find people who don't know the new names you've picked for your animals. Tell them the new name, and then act out the animal and see if they can guess what animal it is!

2. Do like Adam did in our joke, and pick people-names for your five different animals.

3. Ask a friend or family member to rename more animals with you.

THINGS TO TALK ABOUT

1. Do you think it was hard for Adam to name all the animals? Or do you think it was fun?

2. Do you think Adam had a favorite animal?

3. If you were able to have any animal as a pet, what animal would you choose?

HAVE FUN!

Matthew 3:4
John's clothes were made from camel's hair. He wore a leather belt around his waist. For food, he ate locusts and wild honey.

Question
Would you rather wear camel's hair and eat locusts or wear leather and eat wild honey?!

WHAT DID JOHN THE BAPTIST SAY TO THE CAMEL?
NICE OUTFIT.

Matthew 3:4

First, how do you say
Nebuchadnezzar?

neh·buh·kuhd·neh·zr

King Nebuchadnezzar was a Babylonian king who was
mentioned by name over 80 times in the Bible!

You can find his name in five different books of the Bible:
1. 2 Kings
2. 2 Chronicles
3. Jeremiah
4. Ezekiel
5. Daniel

Question
Now ... can you think of anything that actually
does rhyme with Nebuchadnezzar?!

GOD, WHAT RHYMES WITH NEBUCHADNEZZAR?
NO, IT DOESN'T.

Genesis 2:21-22

21 So the Lord God caused the man to sleep very deeply. While the man was asleep, God took one of the ribs from the man's body. Then God closed the man's skin at the place where he took the rib. 22 The Lord God used the rib from the man to make a woman. Then the Lord brought the woman to the man.

Question

Does this scripture make you want to say, "OUCH!"?

WHY DOESN'T EVE LIKE WHEN ADAM LAUGHS TOO HARD?

IT HURTS HIS RIBS.

———

Genesis 2:21-22

Genesis 2:2
By the seventh day God finished the work he had been doing. So on the seventh day he rested from all his work.

Question
Do you catch your dad sleeping...or is he always just "resting his eyes"?!

Did God sleep on the 7th day?
No, He was just resting His eyes.

———

Genesis 2:2

Numbers 22:28
Then the Lord made the donkey talk.
She said to Balaam, "What have I done to
make you hit me three times?"

Question
What would you do if a donkey started
talking to you?!

WHAT DID THE DONKEY SAY TO BALAAM?
QUIT HORSIN' AROUND!

Numbers 22:28

Acts 2:22
"Men of Israel, listen to these words: Jesus from Nazareth was a very special man. God clearly showed this to you by the miracles, wonders, and signs God did through him. You all know this, because it happened right here among you."

Question
What do you think Jesus really likes to eat for lunch?!

What is Jesus's favorite lunch?
Wonder Bread with Miracle Whip.

Acts 2:22

Genesis 2:19-20

[19] From the ground God formed every wild animal and every bird in the sky. He brought them to the man so the man could name them. Whatever the man called each living thing, that became its name. [20] The man gave names to all the tame animals, to the birds in the sky and to all the wild animals. But Adam did not find a helper that was right for him.

Question

Hmm... if you got to name dogs, cats, and giraffes, what do you think you might have called them? Maybe barks, flufflies, and talls?! See the activity on page 8 for more fun naming animals!

WHAT WAS THE FIRST ANIMAL ADAM NAMED?

BOB

———

Genesis 2:19-20

Acts 2:3 (GOD'S WORD Translation)
Tongues that looked like fire appeared to them. The tongues arranged themselves so that one came to rest on each believer.

Question
What do you think you would do if a "tongue of fire" came and rested on your head?!

WHY WERE THE APOSTLES SO THIRSTY IN THE UPPER ROOM?

THEY HAD TONGUES OF FIRE.

Acts 2:3

Matthew 2:11
They went to the house where the child was and saw him with his mother, Mary. They bowed down and worshiped the child. They opened the gifts they brought for him. They gave him treasures of gold, frankincense, and myrrh.

Question
Does your family set up a Nativity Scene at Christmas that includes the three kings bringing their gifts to Jesus? If so, do you think you'll call one of the kings Frank now?!

WHAT DID THE 3 KINGS SAY TO JESUS?
WE HAVE GOLD AND MYRRH, AND FRANK SENT THIS.

―――

Matthew 2:11

This joke is too cheesy to have a Bible reference...

Question
If you got to share cheese with Jesus, which kind would you give Him?!

WHAT IS THE HOLIEST CHEESE?
SWISS CHEESE

This joke is too cheesy to have a Bible reference.

A WHALE OF A TIME

In the Bible, Jonah didn't listen to God and ended up in the belly of a whale for three days until God rescued him. That was probably quite alarming, but what if you could be inside a whale's belly for fun? It's time for you to design a whale and its belly for you to hang out in for three days!

WHAT YOU NEED
1. Paper
2. Coloring utensils
3. Writing utensil

DIRECTIONS

1. First, unlike Jonah, this is a trip you know will end in three days so there's no need to worry! And your whale is make-believe so how it looks, where it swims, and even what its belly is like can be *any way you'd like it to be!*

2. Start by writing down some important things about your whale:

   - Is it a boy or a girl?
   - Does it have a name?
   - How old is it?
   - What color is it? What color is its eyes? What color is its tongue?
   - Does it swim in an ocean, pool, river, or lake?
   - Does it talk? If so, what does it sound like? Does it have an accent?
   - What are its favorite things (for example, song, movie, food)?

3. If you'd like, draw a picture of your whale based on all the things you wrote! If it has a favorite food, song, etc., you can draw those things by it.

4. Now it's time to think about your whale's belly! Just like you did for the whale, write down all the cool things about its belly on your piece of paper. Here are some ideas:

   - Does the belly look like a room in your house or a restaurant or a playground? Think of a place you love to be...that can be what the belly looks like! You can even combine your favorite places.
   - What kinds of fun things are in the belly? Is there a pool table or a pool or a trampoline?
   - Is there a bed where you can sleep or will you stay awake the whole time?
   - Is there a peep hole that you can look through to see where the whale is taking you?
   - Is there food for you to eat?
   - Is there music playing?

5. Keep thinking and writing things down. Remember that you're designing a *really* cool place to stay for three days!

6. If you'd like, draw a picture of your room inside the whale's belly! You can even draw yourself in the room if you'd like.

EXTRA CHALLENGE

Instead of just hanging out in the whale's belly for three days, what if the whale could take you anywhere you wanted to go? Write down some cool places you'd go if you were traveling in the belly of a whale!

THINGS TO TALK ABOUT

1. What is a place in the real world where you'd like to spend three days just hanging out?

2. If you could, would you like to really go inside a whale's belly for three days? If so, would you ask anybody to go with you?

HAVE FUN!

Planet Fassa

For more activities like this, please

SCAN ME!

Jonah 1:17 – 2:1-2, 10
Here is just some of the story of what happened with Jonah and the whale. Make sure to read all of Jonah 2 to see what Jonah prayed.

[17] *And the Lord caused a very big fish to swallow Jonah. Jonah was in the stomach of the fish three days and three nights.*

[2:1] *While Jonah was in the stomach of the fish, he prayed to the Lord his God. Jonah said:* [2] *"I was in danger. So I called to the Lord, and he answered me. I was about to die. So I cried to you, and you heard my voice."* [10] *Then the Lord spoke to the fish. And the fish spit Jonah out of its stomach onto the dry land.*

Question
If you were swallowed by a big whale but knew you'd be out in three days, what would you do in its tummy?! For ideas of what to do, see the activity on page 30.

Why did God save Jonah?
He kept whaling for help.

———

Jonah 2

Matthew 25:32
All the people of the world will be gathered before him. Then he will separate them into two groups as a shepherd separates the sheep from the goats.

Question
If you could grow facial hair, do you think you'd like to grow a beard?!

WHY DIDN'T THE APOSTLES HAVE GOATEES?
BEARDS WERE MUCH MORE SHEEPISH.

———

Matthew 25:32

Genesis 6:15-16, 19-21
Here are just some of the instructions God gave to Noah about building the arc. Make sure to read Genesis 6:13-22 to see all the instructions!

15 "This is how big I want you to build the boat: 450 feet long, 75 feet wide and 45 feet high. 16 Make an opening around the top of the boat. Make it 18 inches high from the edge of the roof down. Put a door in the side of the boat. Make an upper, middle and lower deck in it."

19 "Also, you must bring into the boat two of every living thing, male and female. Keep them alive with you. 20 There will be two of every kind of bird, animal and crawling thing. They will come to you to be kept alive. 21 Also gather some of every kind of food. Store it on the boat as food for you and the animals."

Question
Would you like to be on a boat with two animals of every kind?!

If you ever need help with your boat, I Noah guy.

Genesis 6:13-22

Matthew 14:25-27

25 Between three and six o'clock in the morning, Jesus' followers were still in the boat. Jesus came to them. He was walking on the water. 26 When the followers saw him walking on the water, they were afraid. They said, "It's a ghost!" and cried out in fear. 27 But Jesus quickly spoke to them. He said, "Have courage! It is I! Don't be afraid."

Question
What cool things would you do if you could walk on water like Jesus?!

WHY DID JESUS GET KICKED OFF THE SWIM TEAM?

HE KEPT WALKING ON THE WATER.

Matthew 14:25-27

Genesis 11: 4-5, 7-9
The Tower of Babel was a no-good
mess where people were trying to build
a tower up to reach God! Make sure to read
Genesis 11:1-9 to learn all about it.

^{4} Then they said to each other, "Let's build for ourselves a
city and a tower. And let's make the top of the tower reach high
into the sky. We will become famous. If we do this, we will not be
scattered over all the earth."
^{5} The Lord came down to see the city and the tower that the people
had built. ^{7} [The Lord said] "Come, let us go down and confuse their
language. Then they will not be able to understand each other."
^{8} So the Lord scattered them from there over all the earth. And
they stopped building the city. ^{9} That is where the Lord confused
the language of the whole world. So the place is called Babel.

Question
"Babble" means to make meaningless or silly
sounds. Do you know anyone who
babbles a lot?!

THE TOWER OF BABEL WAS WRONG ON SO MANY LEVELS.

Genesis 11:1-9

Psalm 119:105
Your word is like a lamp for my feet
and a light for my way.

Question
What would you do if your toes could light up like
flashlights?!

WHY DIDN'T THE APOSTLES NEED FLASHLIGHTS?

THE WORD WAS A LAMP TO THEIR FEET.

Psalm 119:105

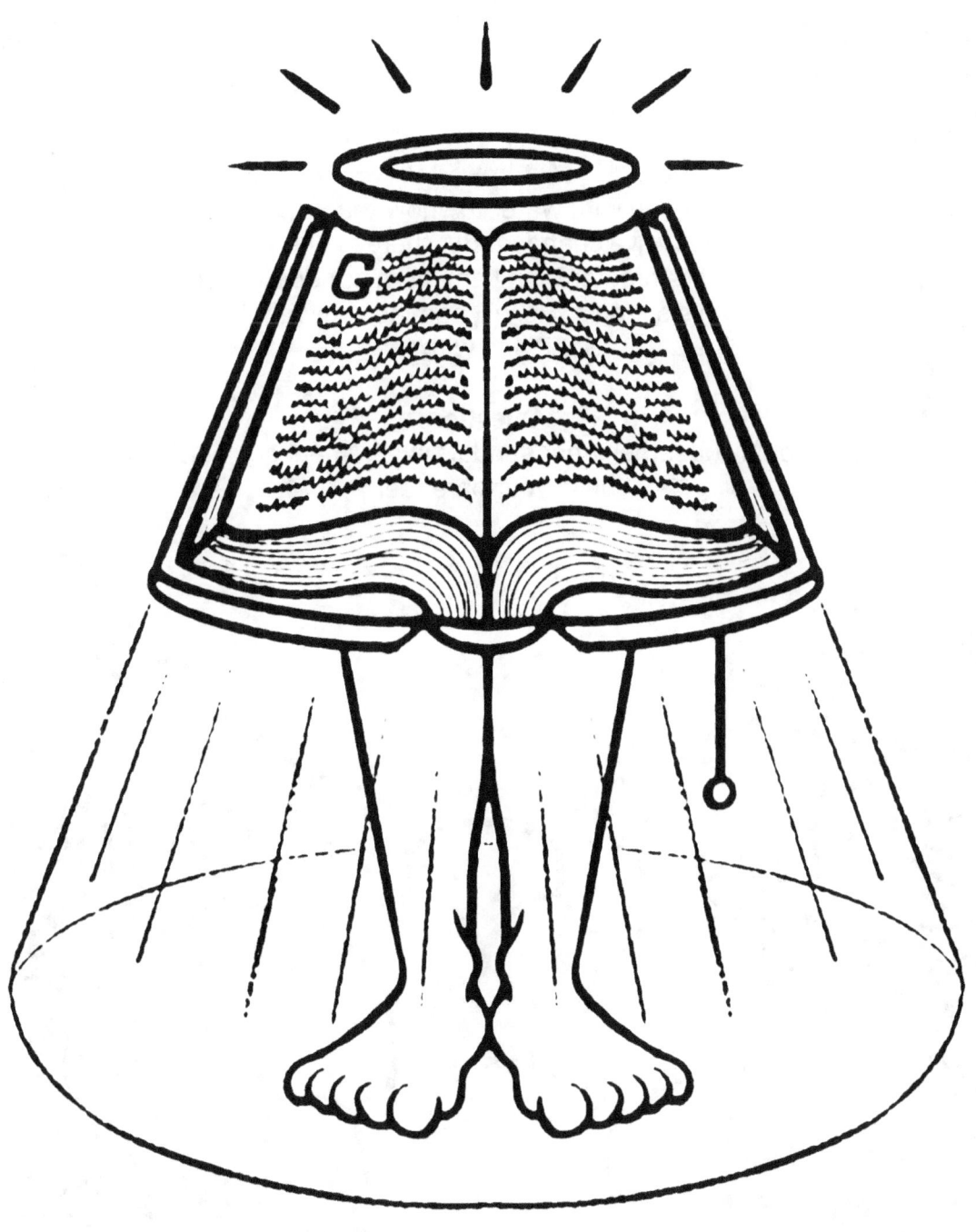

Matthew 3:11
I baptize you with water to show that your hearts and lives have changed. But there is one coming later who is greater than I am. I am not good enough to carry his sandals. He will baptize you with the Holy Spirit and with fire.

Question
Would you rather wear sandals, wear sneakers, or just be in your bare feet?!

WHY DID JESUS LIKE TO WEAR SANDALS?
THEY HAD GOOD SOLES.

Matthew 3:11

2 Corinthians 6:14
You are not the same as those who do not believe. So do not join yourselves to them. Good and bad do not belong together. Light and darkness cannot share together.

Question
A "yoke" is a wooden bar by which two animals like oxen are joined at the heads or necks for working together. Do you think it would be hard to be "yoked" around the neck to someone who is much taller or shorter than you?!

WHY DID THE EGGS BREAK UP?
BECAUSE THEY WERE UNEQUALLY YOKED.

2 Corinthians 6:14

Daniel 3:16-18

[16] Shadrach, Meshach and Abednego answered the king. They said, "Nebuchadnezzar, we do not need to defend ourselves to you. [17] You can throw us into the blazing furnace. The God we serve is able to save us from the furnace and your power. If he does this, it is good. [18] But even if God does not save us, we want you, our king, to know this: We will not serve your gods. We will not worship the gold statue you have set up."

First, can you say all of these names?

Shadrach - **shad·rak**
Meshach - **mee·shak**
Abednego - **uh·bed·nee·go**
Nebuchadnezzar - **neh·buh·kuhd·neh·zr**

Question
Do you like spicey food? If yes, what is your favorite spicey food to eat?!

WHAT'S JESUS'S FAVORITE SPICE BLEND?
SHADRACH, MESHACH, AND OREGANO.

Daniel 3:16-18

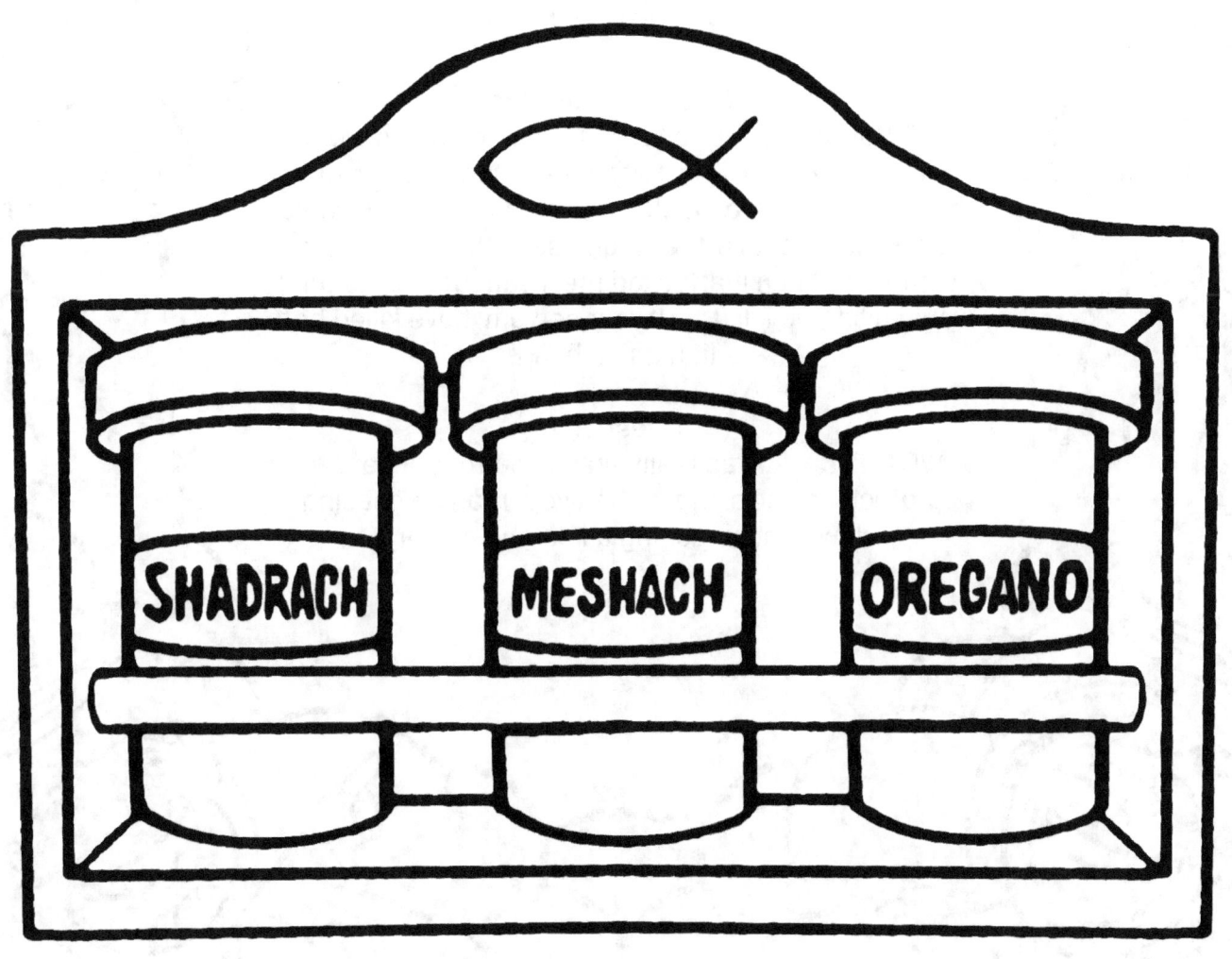

1 Samuel 17:34-36a

³⁴ But David said to Saul, "I, your servant, have been keeping my father's sheep. When a lion or bear came and took a sheep from the flock, ³⁵ I would chase it. I would attack it and save the sheep from its mouth. When it attacked me, I caught it by its fur. I would hit it and kill it. ³⁶ᵃ I, your servant, have killed both a lion and a bear!"

Question

WOAH!! David was really brave and fought hard to protect his dad's sheep! Can you imagine chasing down and wrestling a lion and a bear?!

BELIEVE ME! DAVID WRESTLED A BEAR! THAT'S NO LION, MAN.

1 Samuel 17:34–36a

Daniel 6:16, 19-22
Here is just some of the story of what happened to Daniel. Make sure to read all of Daniel 6 to see how God saved Daniel from the lions!

16 *So King Darius gave the order. They brought Daniel and threw him into the lions' den. The king said to Daniel, "May the God you serve all the time save you!"*
19 *The next morning King Darius got up at dawn. He hurried to the lions' den.* 20 *As he came near the den, he was worried. He called out to Daniel. He said, "Daniel, servant of the living God! Has your God that you always worship been able to save you from the lions?"*
21 *Daniel answered, "My king, live forever!* 22 *My God sent his angel to close the lions' mouths. They have not hurt me, because my God knows I am innocent. I never did anything wrong to you, my king."*

Question
When you are afraid of things, knowing that Jesus and the angels are with you can make things so much better! Can you think of one thing that makes you worried, afraid, or nervous? Now tell it to GO AWAY because Jesus is your friend, and He won't let that thing bother you anymore!

WHAT ROOM DOES DANIEL TRY TO AVOID?
THE DEN

———

Daniel 6

Judges 16:19
Delilah got Samson to go to sleep. He was lying in her lap. Then she called in a man to shave off the seven braids of Samson's hair. In this way she began to make him weak. And Samson's strength left him.

Question
It sure wasn't nice for Delilah to cut Samson's hair! Do you like to get your hair cut?!

DID YOU HEAR THE ONE ABOUT SAMSON AND DELILAH?

IT WAS A HAIRY SITUATION.

———

Judges 16:19

Acts 5:27-28
To be "on the lam" is to be "on the run," actively escaping from an enemy.

The apostles got in trouble all the time for teaching about Jesus, but they didn't care because they knew He is awesome, and they wanted to tell everyone about Him, just like we do! If you want to learn more, read Acts 5:17-42.

[27] The soldiers brought the apostles to the meeting and made them stand before the Jewish leaders. The high priest questioned them. [28] He said, "We gave you strict orders not to go on teaching in that name. But look what you have done! You have filled Jerusalem with your teaching. You are trying to make us responsible for this man's death."

Question
People ride on horses, mules, camels, and elephants, but not usually on lambs! If you could take a ride on any animal, which one would you choose?!

WHAT HAPPENED WHEN THE APOSTLES TAUGHT THE GOSPEL?
THEY WERE CONSTANTLY ON THE LAMB.

Acts 5:17-42

Matthew 5:13-16

[13] "You are the salt of the earth. But if the salt loses its salty taste, it cannot be made salty again. It is good for nothing. It must be thrown out for people to walk on. [14] You are the light that gives light to the world. A city that is built on a hill cannot be hidden. [15] And people don't hide a light under a bowl. They put the light on a lampstand. Then the light shines for all the people in the house. [16] In the same way, you should be a light for other people. Live so that they will see the good things you do. Live so that they will praise your Father in heaven."

Question

As Jesus says, YOU are the light of the world! What color light are you?!

What is Jesus' favorite type of popcorn?
Light and salty

Matthew 5:13-16

LIGHT & SALTY

I'd Go Anywhere for You

In the Bible, a group of four friends carried their good buddy all the way up to a roof and lowered him through it so he could be healed by Jesus! What a great group of friends. Now it's time for you to imagine a cool thing you'd do for your best friend!

WHAT YOU NEED
1. Paper or see page 77
2. Coloring utensils
3. Writing utensil

DIRECTIONS

1. Think about your best friend. This could be a sibling, a neighbor, a classmate, or even your mom, dad, grandma, or grandpa!

2. Think of three things this person likes the most. You can write these things down or just say them out loud. It can be things like his or her favorite food, movie, sport, activity, or pet. If you can't think of three things, you can ask your friend. (But don't tell your friend why you're asking!)

3. Now choose one of the three things you listed.

4. On page 77 or a separate piece of paper, you are going to draw your best friend's favorite thing! But first, as you can see on page 77, it says, "I would go to _____ and back to get you _____." Before you draw your picture, fill that in. (Or you can write the whole sentence yourself on your own piece of paper.)

   In the first blank space, write down somewhere fun or far or silly. In the second blank space, write down your best friend's favorite thing. Here are some examples:

   - I would go to <u>the moon</u> and back to get you <u>spaghetti</u>.
   - I would go to <u>school</u> and back to get you <u>your dog</u>.
   - I would go to <u>the zoo</u> and back to get you <u>your sweater</u>.

   Make up a fun or silly place you'd be willing to go just to get your best friend the thing he or she likes most!

5. After you write your sentence, draw your wonderful picture.

6. Make your best friend's day by giving him or her your drawing!

EXTRA CHALLENGES

1. Do a second drawing for another person you really love.

2. Instead of just drawing your friend's favorite thing, also draw a picture of you going to get it. For example, if you said you'd go to the moon to get spaghetti, you can draw yourself on the moon getting spaghetti!

THINGS TO TALK ABOUT

1. You wrote down the three things your best friend likes the most. What are the three you like the most?

2. You wrote down a fun or silly place you'd go just to get your best friend's item. Why did you choose that place?

3. It's so wonderful to have a best friend. Adults: talk about one of the best friends you had when you were a child and what you two loved to do together.

HAVE FUN!

Planet Fassa

For more activities like this, please

SCAN ME!

Mark 2:3-4

³ Some people came, bringing a paralyzed man to Jesus. Four of them were carrying the paralyzed man. ⁴ But they could not get to Jesus because of the crowd. So they went to the roof above Jesus and made a hole in the roof. Then they lowered the mat with the paralyzed man on it.

Question

These are pretty awesome friends who really loved each other. Can you name four people that you love?! See the activity on page 60 to help you think of people you love.

WHAT DID THE MAN SAY TO JESUS WHEN HE WAS LOWERED THROUGH THE ROOF?

SORRY TO DROP IN ON YOU ...

Mark 2:3-4

A basic act of hospitality in Biblical times was to wash one's feet before entering a house because wearing sandals caused feet to become very dirty.

Question
Do you like when your feet are muddy or do you like to clean them off right away?!

Knock, knock.
Who's there?
Orange.
Orange who?
Orange you glad I washed my feet?

———

A basic act of hospitality in Biblical times was to wash one's feet before entering a house because wearing sandals caused feet to become very dirty.

Joshua 5:6
The Israelites had moved about in the desert for 40 years. During that time all the fighting men who had left Egypt had died. This was because they had not obeyed the Lord. So the Lord swore they would not see the land. This was the land he had promised their ancestors to give them. It was a land where much food grows.

Question
Oh no! It is no fun when you are lost. Have you ever gotten lost before?!

WHY DID THE ISRAELITES WANDER IN THE DESERT FOR SO LONG?
THEY DIDN'T FOLLOW THE SIGNS.

———

Joshua 5:6

THIS WAY TO THE PROMISED LAND

2 Kings 13:20-21

[20] So Elisha died and was buried. At that time groups of Moabites would rob the land in the springtime. [21] Once the Israelites were burying a man. Suddenly they saw a group of Moabites coming. The Israelites threw the dead man into Elisha's grave. When the man touched Elisha's bones, the man came back to life. And he stood up on his feet.

Question

Are you old enough to wake up to an alarm clock yet? If so, do you need it to be really LOUD or does a soft sound wake you up?!

WHY WERE ELISHA'S BONES SO ALARMING?
THEY SURE WOKE THAT GUY UP!

2 Kings 13:20-21

Holy Spirit really likes clean sheets.
You would too if you were the Comforter.

———

John 14:16-17

Remember that Holy Spirit likes clean sheets?
You would too if you were the Holy Ghost.

———

John 14:16-17

John 14:16-17

¹⁶ I will ask the Father, and he will give you another Helper. He will give you this Helper to be with you forever. ¹⁷ The Helper is the Spirit of truth. The world cannot accept him because it does not see him or know him. But you know him. He lives with you and he will be in you.

Question
It looks like the Holy Spirit likes clean sheets. Do you think He likes it when you make your bed too?!

Exodus 8:1-19

In Exodus 8:1-19, the Bible tells about the plagues of gnats and frogs that came onto the Egyptians because Pharaoh would NOT listen to what God was telling Moses! To read about all the plagues that happened in Egypt, read Exodus 7:14 - 11.

Question

Having frogs and gnats everywhere would definitely be gross. If you had to choose one animal, bug, or reptile to rain down from the sky, what would you choose?!

WHEN IT'S RAINING CATS AND DOGS, I THINK OF EGYPT AND THANK GOD IT'S NOT GNATS AND FROGS!

Exodus 8:1-19

John 1:29
The next day John saw Jesus coming toward him.
John said, "Look, the Lamb of God. He takes away the
sins of the world!"

Question
What is your favorite activity to do with Jesus? Is it
dancing, singing, swimming, karate?!

WHAT'S JESUS'S FAVORITE KARATE MOVE?
THE LAMB CHOP

John 1:29

Give thanks to the LORD, for He is good;
His love endures forever.
—
Psalm 107:1

A joyful heart is good medicine.
—
Proverbs 17:22

In Your presence is fullness of joy.
—
Psalm 16:11

I WOULD GO _____

AND BACK TO GET YOU _____

www.ingramcontent.com/pod-product-compliance
Lightning Source LLC
Chambersburg PA
CBHW081723120626

46550CB00010B/3229